AF521892

The Art of Susan Rios

by Ralph Rugoff

Hugh Lauter Levin Associates, Inc.
New York
Distributed by
Macmillan Publishing Company

ISBN: 0-88363-587-9

Printed in Japan

Dustjacket:
Front: *Visiting* (detail) *1984*
Back: *Romance Suite*
First Love, 1987
From This Day Forward, 1987
The New Arrival, 1987
Attic Memories, 1987

Contents

Foreword

In the ensuing pages, author and art critic Ralph Rugoff explores the style, the content, and the history of the art of Susan Rios. Sitting down to write this introduction, it occurs to me that between these covers there is a wealth of information about an artist and her work, information and imagery that establish an important role for Susan Rios in the world of contemporary fine art.

For the newcomer discovering Susan Rios for the first time through the pages of this book, and for the knowledgeable patron who already loves and collects her work, *The Art of Susan Rios* is a docent tour that will entertain, inform, and enlighten its audience.

Rugoff has managed the difficult task of revealing the artist's thinking and feeling processes before and after she creates a canvas. While this may be an interesting approach to learning about any artist, it is especially important with Rios, because that is what her work is all about: thinking and feeling.

Says Rugoff: "Rios...presents realistic physical environments in her paintings, but her direct appeal is to our hearts and minds. This is what gives them the power to set us dreaming." Stand before any painting, drawing, or serigraph by Susan Rios and you will know what he means. In each and every image she is able to capture the prevailing mood: a feeling, an emotion, a situation, a time and place. What comes to mind is not only the beautiful scenery, the intricate interiors of homes or the charm of a garden path–but more important than that, you invariably get the feeling that you know what it's like to be there. Something inherently human has been translated to canvas and paint. You can sense the emotion, though no one is there. You can feel the warmth and vitality and even the excitement of being there...finding total peace with yourself or sharing it with the one you love.

I've often thought how wonderful it would be to spend a summer alone with just my family, inhabiting the places that Susan Rios paints. It's an "Alice-in-Wonderland" fantasy of course, but I believe it's that same fantasy in all of us that has made Susan Rios so popular and so appealing to people in all walks of life. There is no doubt that Susan Rios has a gift. Her thought-provoking interiors and vividly colored exteriors resound with it; but more important, she has something to give. Her art is a gust of fresh air in a fast-paced high-tech world; a window out from the pressure and stress of the 1980s.

In just the five years or so that Martin Lawrence Limited Editions has been publishing Susan Rios, I have watched her market grow to worldwide proportion. Susan Rios's works can now be seen in 48 of the 50 states; in 1986 we began distributing her works in Japan and Canada; in 1987 in England, Taiwan, and Hong Kong. What lies ahead for Susan Rios is certain to include success, fame and fortune–and also certain to include a very real sense of what else people need in this day and age: humanity, serenity, and romance. Her medium and her message speak directly to the quality of life.

Martin S. Blinder
Publisher
Martin Lawrence Limited Editions, Inc.

Susan Rios Self-Portrait, 1979
Acrylic, 30 x 30"

My Journal

The Art of Susan Rios

by Ralph Rugoff

Few contemporary artists convey the profound tranquility and peaceful beauty that imbue the paintings of Susan Rios. And even fewer artists are capable of evoking the warmth and intimacy that radiate from a Rios canvas. Susan Rios's images invite us into a cozily circumscribed sphere of experience and engage us in a private dialogue about the most important things in life: friendship, family, a sense of self, and a feeling of home.

In person, Susan Rios is an open-hearted, bright-eyed woman whose features bear a marked resemblance to those of the actress Kathleen Turner. Along with her husband Jon Zegel and her daughter Olivia, the 37-year-old Rios lives in a sleepy Los Angeles suburb, the quiet streets of which are lined with colonnades of towering palm trees. Like the interiors she is so fond of painting, Rios's own home neatly combines turn-of-the-century elegance with a more rustic, down-home ambiance. Rios herself immediately puts one at ease with her unpretentious charm and ingenuous cordiality. Whether sitting at her dining room table freely recounting her life story, or working in her studio on her latest painting, Susan Rios's sincerity and warmth are readily apparent.

Rios successfully expresses these same qualities in her art. Her paintings evince a loving attention to intimate details and a concern for the small things in life that contribute to the character of the whole. In her 1986 painting *Amaryllis, Too,* Rios characteristically creates an environment where almost anyone would feel instantly at home. Rios's skills as a colorist are clearly evident in this work: the living room hums with friendly tones and lively patterns in a complex composition that would strain the talents of many artists. Yet Rios's extreme sensitivity to nuance of hue enables her to create a carefully orchestrated symphony of color. Subtle shades of pink, mauve, and rose play off one another in the floral motifs ingeniously echoed throughout the room, from the framed painting tucked away on a back wall to the amaryllis in the foreground to which the title refers. Despite a certain visual busyness, the color scheme remains subdued enough to allow the scene to exude a homey tranquility. And when contrasted to the silvery gray light and cold cloudy skies appearing in the two windows, the warmth of the interior tableau becomes all the more inviting.

Rios's delicate use of line invests *Amaryllis, Too* with a mellifluous grace. The sinuous curves of the furniture link the lower half of the painting in a pleasing visual

The Last Dance (detail)

The nearly four-year-old Susan Rios appears delighted with her Christmas treasures, December 1953.

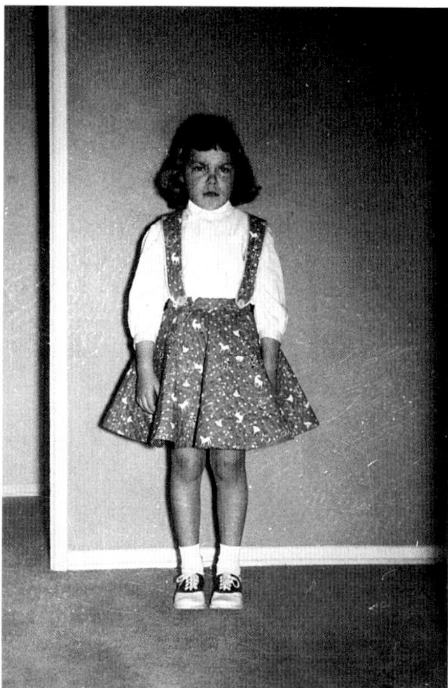

Susan Rios getting ready for her first day of kindergarten. September 1955, Reseda, California.

rhythm punctuated by the gently sensuous contours of the floral imagery. As in most of Rios's compositions, there are no hard edges in this work: straight lines inevitably tend to buckle slightly, converging according to the whims of a shifting perspective or the topography of a fluffily plump pillow. The result is a dulcet sense of harmony in the overall composition.

Rios delights in rendering the specific texture of surfaces and objects in her paintings. With her eloquently restrained brush stroke, Rios perfectly captures the sway of a flower stem and the grain of an oak door. In *Amaryllis, Too,* the pillows on the couch are carefully modeled to suggest volume, while the tea service resting on the chest in the middle of the room is gradually shaded so that it stands out from the background. Rios's attention to articulating the different surface textures of each and every object complements her excellent eye for atmospheric detail. When one observes a Rios picture, it seems impossible to imagine that anything is missing from the scene. More than any simple visual realism, it is this characteristic completeness that enables a Rios canvas to convey the feel of a given place perfectly. "What satisfies me most in life are the little things, like watching my roses bloom or observing a butterfly," remarks the artist with a smile. "So in my paintings, I try to work from the small details to build a similiar feeling. It's those little details that give you the sense of being right there."

In many of Rios's interiors, her recurring motifs—blue-and-white china, handsomely bound books, cozy wicker furniture, and elegant lace tablecloths—also serve to indicate a particular milieu. Through decorative detail she portrays what amounts to a philosophy of life: the Victorian elegance and bucolic comfort of the environments she depicts speak for rest rather than change, contemplation and quiet conversation rather than impetuous movement and frivolity.

In addition, Rios employs details—such as a ribboned hat or a pair of shoes—to suggest the presence and activities of characters who remain unseen, positioned outside the boundaries of the picture frame. Yet Rios's richly detailed locations allow us to imagine just what these men and women must be like—people it would be wonderful to sit down with for a long heart-to-heart talk.

This oblique narrative strategy is exemplified in the 1985 painting *That Delightful Chat.* Two brown wicker chairs face each other as if positioned to accommodate an intimate tête-à-tête, while the two tea cups and the lone volume suggest a leisurely afternoon discussion of literature and art. In one sense the painting seems to represent absence as much as any specific presence, since no actual conversationalists are depicted. Instead, Rios leaves us with the evidence of their activity and invites us to reconstruct a past scene from the clues before us. The draped bust in the background can be seen as a surrogate for the missing human protagonists as well as a reference to the general topic of art. From this point of view, the painting seems suffused with the warm, quiet afterglow that follows a wonderful conversation with a close friend.

By omitting the human figure from most of her images, Rios gives the viewer license to fill in the narrative details: the stage is dressed for a particular genre, but the specifics of the drama are left to the viewer's imagination. The two unoccupied chairs featured in *That Delightful Chat*—typically rendered with Rios's exacting craftsmanship—seem invitingly vacant; they tempt us to enjoy our own private fantasy by projecting ourselves into the depicted scene. "If a figure is shown in a painting, you're locked into a very specific reading of the image," Rios notes. "I usually choose to leave human figures out of my paintings so that people can put whatever they want of themselves into them."

The open-ended narrativity of Rios's work is certainly one factor that has contributed to her enthusiastic reception. Because they are designed to encourage the creative participation of the viewer, her paintings are more truly a form of interactive art than much of the contemporary work aspiring to that claim. We find in Susan Rios's idyllic scenes the opportunity to escape from the cares of the moment; we can take delight in picturing ourselves sharing a quiet interchange in a picturesque Rios garden or parlor and leaving behind the rushed and jagged rhythms of our fast-food culture.

Despite the absence of human figures, a Rios painting never seems empty or lonely. With her expressive use of detail, Susan Rios manages to suggest that people have either just left the scene or are just about to return to resume some interrupted activity. Part of the reason Rios can so effectively convey this atmosphere is that she often proceeds from a specific narrative idea or characterization, which colors the mood of a given scene for her. "I tend to develop stories in my mind as I'm working on a painting, and I'll add details to illustrate it," she observes. "For instance, with my 1986 painting *The Last Dance,* I began to imagine a scenario involving a young girl who had just been to a dance. On the table are the pearls she had borrowed from her mother. She has just been sitting in this room, thinking about the dance and reading her journal. The romantic picture on the back wall was added simply to suggest the general theme." The result is an evocative suggestion of human presence and activity.

Susan Rios was born in 1950, in Terre Haute, Indiana. After a mere three years as a Hoosier, she moved with her family to southern California. A childhood love of the outdoors led her to begin drawing scenes from nature, and at the age of 13, she was awarded a scholarship to a summer art program at California State University at Northridge. "I was always daydreaming as a child," Rios recalls. "That's where I got my comfort from, and my drawings grew out of that use of my imagination."

After several years of college, she found employment in a flower shop. It was a job that proved to be an ideal preparation for her future career as a painter. Starting at the modest salary of fifty cents an hour, Rios worked on and off at the shop for five years. "It was good training because it brought out my natural creative abilities," Rios said. "I did everything from wedding bouquets to funeral sprays. In terms of learning how to blend colors, it was the best training I could have had."

A love of flowers nurtured by her work in the flower shop is evident in Susan Rios's paintings. Featured in teeming gardens, elegant vases, and appearing as decorative motifs in the design of rugs, wallpaper, and upholstery fabric, flowers are a significant element in most Rios compositions. Unlike the floral designs of many other artists working in similar genres, Rios's flowers always seem uncannily vivid and true to life. This is partly due to Rios's exacting draftsmanship—her meticulous modeling of each and every petal and stem ensures that each flower stands out as a distinctly individual creation. But what most distinguishes Rios from her contemporaries is her unerring sense of color—her ability to find the precise blend of lavender and violet, for instance, to employ in painting a morning glory. It's a talent that Rios has honed with a disciplined practice of empirical observation.

"I can look at something if I'm interested and know immediately what colors I'm going to have to use to get there," Rios declares. "Very seldom do I use paint straight from the tube. Most of the time, I blend colors to achieve exactly the shade I'm looking for and then build up layers of color upon color to achieve the right undertones. If I'm painting a dark background, I'll use five or six layers of color, building up from the darker tones, to get the intensity I'm looking for."

In garden scenes, such as the 1986 canvas *Garden Memories,* the composition is dictated as much by Rios's use of color as by conventional perspective. The lower half of the painting displays Rios's exquisite ability to orchestrate color: a wide spectrum of shades and tones are subtly organized into a complex composition made to appear

That Delightful Chat, 1985
Acrylic, 34 x 30″

The Last Dance, 1986
Acrylic, 28 x 28"

Susan and daughter Olivia Rios, then ten years of age, pose for wedding portraits.

A wedding portrait of Susan Rios and Jon Zegel.

casually spontaneous. This naturalistic handling recalls the approach of the nineteenth-century Impressionists, who rejected the restrictive visual grammar of classical painting and instead strove to capture the freshness and intuitive gestalt of first impressions. Certainly, Susan Rios's buoyant palette owes a debt to the pioneers of plein air painting, yet overall, the realistic accents of her work place it apart from the Impressionist camp. For all its overgrown lushness, the scene shown in *Garden Memories* is rendered without sacrificing integrity of line. Rios's technical balancing act is mirrored thematically by her subject: the garden is represented as embodying both nature (the untamed fecundity of the foreground flora) and culture (the harmony of the garden's architectural design, visible in the upper third of the canvas).

There is a decidedly feminine sensibility at work in the paintings of Susan Rios. Her delicate rendering of flowers, and her fondness for depicting elegant interiors replete with china tea sets and lace tablecloths, highlight a softness of touch traditionally associated with the world of women. So it is worth noting that Susan Rios traces the genesis of her career to the period following the birth of her daughter Olivia. "After Olivia was born, I quit my job at the flower shop," Rios relates. "I stayed home and questioned myself. I knew I had an ability I wasn't taking advantage of, and if I couldn't even believe in myself, I had to wonder what I could possibly give to my child. Having Olivia refocused my life."

Susan Rios first found an outlet for her talents by creating her own greeting cards, and shortly afterward she made her first attempts at painting. Confident that she had found her calling, Rios began working in a studio in Santa Monica. Yet in the midst of her excitement at launching a career in the arts, Rios found herself drawn ever closer to her newborn daughter. "When I first began to paint, Olivia was just an infant," Rios recalls. "Seeing her quietly asleep created warm and tender emotions, and those feelings assumed a much greater importance for me. I set out to discover and release those emotions in my work."

The "feminine touch" in Rios's work is ultimately romantic rather than maternal, however; indeed, this may be one reason why her paintings apppeal to men as much as to women. In contrast to the Hollywood fantasy of glamorous passion, Rios's concept of romance is centered around the cultivation of an atmosphere of intimacy. The quietly contemplative scenes Rios depicts seem ideal spots for promoting a feeling of closeness and a shared exploration of self.

Rios's abiding interest in investing her work with a strongly personal appeal is a concern she shares with two

Amaryllis, Too, 1986
Acrylic, 40 x 50″

Susan Rios at work in her studio (Los Angeles, 1987).

great Post-Impressionist painters, Edouard Vuillard (1868–1940) and Pierre Bonnard (1867–1947). Like Rios, both Vuillard and Bonnard often painted scenes featuring the calm beauty of summer gardens and the quiet domesticity of warmly lit interiors. Because of their extremely personal interpretations of these subjects, Vuillard and Bonnard were referred to as "Intimists." While the compositions of both generally included human figures, the importance of these figures was usually marginal. Instead, the paintings tended to focus on small details such as a bowl of fruit, a pile of old books, or a vase of flowers, transforming these traditionally insignificant elements into the warm, subtly vibrating heart of the work.

In particular, Vuillard's paintings of the 1920s seem to anticipate some of Susan Rios's most striking traits. Executed on a small scale, Vuillard's interiors from this period principally draw their character from the furniture, textiles, and flowers he so lovingly painted. His domestic scenes were inevitably cluttered with detail: elegant lamps, busts, stacks of worn books, and patterned textiles of every description. Rather than suggesting specific narrative content, Vuillard's details contributed to building up the resonant intimacy that suffused his scenes. As does Rios today, Vuillard excelled in evoking a sense of place so that the viewer immediately experienced the *personality* of a given room as if it were a living thing.

Like the individualistic Intimists and their Impressionist predecessors, Susan Rios seems to view the world through a special lens. In her paintings, she sees art as a creative process of filtering and transforming. The subject of a Rios painting is not simply what is shown on the canvas, but also includes this distillation process; the final image Rios presents is the record and trace of a thinking and deeply feeling eye.

Susan Rios recalls that she first became aware of this aspect of art-making while taking a drawing class at Pierce College. "The instructor had us doing continuous line drawings, and it really got me to realize that art is teaching yourself how to see things," observed Rios. "You can't really teach someone how to create art—you can expose them to technique and art history, but ultimately, what you create comes from your own imagination and your own filter system."

Rios's "filter system"—the unique sensibility through which she interprets the world—endows each of her works with a distinctive style, a trademark look. Yet however much of herself Susan Rios puts into her paintings, her images are not impenetrably personal or eccentric. Instead, they greet us with an immediate sense of recognition; they seem saturated with familiarity. For example, the 1985 painting *Cape May* inevitably reminds viewers of somewhere they already know: a town where they grew up, a treasured summer vacation spot, the site of an unforgettable visit. It might remind one person of Martha's Vineyard, another of a small town in Wisconsin, while a third person might insist it's an actual street in Carmel. But each viewer feels he or she already possesses an intimate knowledge of the place depicted.

By blending imagination and memory with specific pictorial elements from documentary sources, Rios assembles an idealized image. While *Cape May* was in fact inspired by a visit to the real town of that name on the New Jersey shore, Rios's painting is not a reproduction of any specific street. Instead, Rios employs readily recognizable details—such as the two American flags, the Victorian gingerbread architecture, the lambent play of light and shadow on the lawn and sidewalk—to evoke the quintessence of small town America on a serene midsummer Sunday. The result seems instantly identifiable because of its archetypal qualities rather than because it is an image of some actual place familiar to the viewer.

One conspicuous aspect of Rios's creative filtering is that her paintings consistently leave out any references to modern technology. There are no telephones, electric lights, quartz alarm clocks, or personal computers in any of Rios's images. This absence of post-industrial artifacts seems directed in part toward re-creating the aura of some earlier era of gracious living when the rhythms of daily life were composed to a more natural measure.

Rios, however, insists that her exclusion of technology represents a conscious decision that supports the overall effect she is interested in achieving. "It's not that I'm striving to evoke a nostalgic atmosphere of some earlier period of time," she explains. "It's simply that showing a modern lamp or a television set wouldn't fit in with the romantic mood I want to create. What I try to do," Rios elaborates, "is portray things that could be from any time period. So if I paint a wicker chair, for instance, it could be that it's an antique in a modern home, or it might just as easily be a brand new chair in a nineteenth-century home." In this manner Rios strategically circumvents any attempt to lock her scenes into a narrowly defined historical reality. By maintaining an indefinite time reference, the narrative element in Rios's paintings retains maximum elasticity and remains wide open to the viewer's imagination.

The extent to which Rios's own imagination is at work in her paintings becomes evident upon a visit to her studio. Neither a sunlit Victorian parlor nor a romantically sprawling loft, Rios's studio is a neatly organized space that includes high-tech accents inconceivable in a Rios painting. But as Rios herself is quick to point out, the content of her work is not directly autobiographical. "People are under the mistaken impression that, because I can paint the kind of scenes I do, I spend my whole life in some kind of dream world. But my paintings are largely works of the imagination—they represent idealized situations and not necessarily what I'm actually feeling when I'm working on them."

Susan Rios is a prolific artist. She claims that it takes her an average of only two and one-half weeks to complete an entire painting. Considering the wealth of detailed imagery in her work and the fact that her paintings often contain as many as sixty different color shadings, Rios's speed is all the more remarkable. Rios explains that she rarely executes thumbnail sketches of a subject, but instead begins painting after drawing in a rough outline of the composition on canvas.

Rios's use of fast-drying acrylic paints further facilitates her technical celerity. Because they combine pigment with an emulsion of plastic and water, acrylics dry as quickly as do water colors—when the water evaporates on exposure to air, the plastic particles bond to form a hard waterproof paint. "Working with acrylics, I can paint nonstop; I never have to leave an idea for another day. With oils, I always found myself waiting for the paint to dry, and that interfered with the flow of my creative energy. Acrylics also enable me to work more exactly," she continues. "They allow me full use of my overpainting technique. And the colors are wonderful."

Because she generally works on an intimate scale, Rios favors small brushes, which allow her precision in painting the intricate patterns that so often show up in her compositions. In the 1987 *From This Day Forward* (part of her "Romance Suite"), Rios presents the viewer with a panoply of complex surface design. The composition comprises an elaborate exercise in geometric abstraction just as much as it represents a realistic still life: the delicate weave of the lace bedspread; the complicated, multicolored mosaic of the rug; the floral print of the background wallpaper; and the stunning burst of color captured in the bridal bouquet all combine to fill every square inch of canvas with an impressive array of abstract designs.

Retreat, a 1986 canvas, similiarly displays Rios's penchant for painting patterns. Each piece of china in the scene is individually characterized with a distinct and elegantly executed design motif. Other details, such as the ornately braided lace drapery, the vibrant blue-and-white checked divan cover, and the strongly defined wood grain on the side table, provide discrete areas of visual complex-

Cape May, 1985
Acrylic, 30 x 24″

Garden Memories, 1986
Acrylic, 24 x 30″

Susan Rios, 1987.

Susan Rios's home near Los Angeles is very much like her paintings. Wicker and lace, flowers and pillows create an atmosphere that is a unique blend of Victorian grace and California country.

ity that augment the overall compositional dynamics with their direct appeal to the viewer's eye. In this respect, Rios's work recalls the paintings of the seventeenth-century Dutch artist Vermeer, who similarly delighted in depicting richly patterned oriental rugs, colorful tablecloths, vivid tiles, and lush drapery. As with Rios's work today, Vermeer's realistic scenes were thus given an abstract, architectural edge. Yet with both artists, fascination with pattern never springs from purely decorative intent; the care and attention lavished on intricate details invest them with a dramatic and emotional value that enhances the overall thematic concerns.

The abstract element provided by Rios's use of pattern is complemented by the shifting perspective evident in much of her work. Planes of space often seem to shift in a Rios painting; objects within a single scene may be shown from varying vantage points. Rios's fluid perspective lends her images a dreamy quality that hints of surrealism. The scenes depicted in Rios's paintings seem to exist in glass-bubble worlds where the laws of realism work side by side with the play of the imagination.

Perhaps the salient trait of Rios's work is the insular quality that characterizes her images. The environments Rios presents are peaceful sanctuaries cloistered from the so-called real world. A scene like that shown in the 1984 painting, *Thoughts on a Happy Ending,* appears cloaked in an all-enveloping privacy, and the resulting suggestion of silence and spellbinding stillness has an almost hypnotic effect on the viewer. Rios perfectly evokes the kind of cozy atmosphere where one feels comfortably alone and that special mood in which the writings of a favorite author and one's own reflections are more than adequate company.

Ultimately, Rios's paintings present themselves as metaphors for states of mind. Regardless of their visual subject matter, Rios's images are inevitably saturated with psychological content. Rather than directing the viewer to an interpretation of nature or interior design, these idealized tableaux seem to refer back to the painter's own imagination and inner emotional life. This is what gives them the power to set us dreaming—they welcome us to that baffling mental playground where the most important part of our existence is lived. Rios similarly presents realistic physical environments in her paintings, but her direct appeal is to our hearts and minds.

Underlying all the many facets of Susan Rios's art is a strong humanistic emphasis. Her paintings emanate life-affirming values. When we look at them, we instinctively feel better—about ourselves and about the possibilities for the world we live in. That Susan Rios's work succeeds in this manner testifies to the integrity of her talent. Any artist concerned with portraying universal emotions risks cliché, and it is only those capable of resolutely following their personal vision who manage to transcend triteness. Rios is just such an artist. Her art overflows with sentiment, but it is never sentimental.

Nowhere is this more apparent than when Rios treats the theme of romance. Typically, Rios never shows us the lovers themselves, yet in each picture a distinct drama unfolds. An idyllic picnic scene is featured in *First Love,* part of Rios's 1987 "Romance Suite" series. A blanket lies stretched out on an inviting spot of grass, nestled under a leafy tree. With a few telling details—an open book of poetry, a bouquet, a flower-bedecked summer hat—Rios sets the stage for a romantic luncheon. The narrow stream in the background leads the viewer's eyes off into the distance, where it is easy to imagine a pair of lovers walking hand in hand. There is an innocent lyricism to the scene that successfully conjures up feelings linked to the painting's title.

In *From This Day Forward,* Rios focuses on a few specific details. A bridal bouquet and what may be part of the bridal veil appear to have been casually deposited on the corner of a frilly lace wedding bed. A pair of white shoes nonchalantly rests on the patterned rug. It is an image redolent of traditional femininity, recalling the old nursery rhyme that girls are made of sugar and spice and everything nice. Yet this delicate tapestry of detail also exudes a tenderness that bespeaks the highest form of romance. One can have no doubt that the owner of those white shoes will make a wonderful wife.

Rios's paintings chart the course of true romance through progressive stages. In *The New Arrival,* a family of teddy bears stand in for their human counterparts. A child's clothing hangs next to a painting of a woman affectionately fondling a rabbit. The cheerfully decorative scheme of the room assures us that the new arrival has been warmly welcomed. The scope of the original romance has been broadened to accommodate a growing family, and while the tone of this picture necessarily marks a change from that of the preceding two canvases, it grows out of their spirit. The fourth painting in this series, *Attic Memories* evokes the fruits of a happy marriage by depicting a scene of nostalgic recollections. The cozily cloistered interior is an idealized setting for reviewing the wedding pictures, family photographs, and poignant moments of a treasured past. Rios's painting successfully suggests the inner satisfaction one experiences in such activity.

In *The Golden Years,* Rios presents another idealized vision of a fully matured relationship. Behind a curtain of garden flowers in the foreground, two comfortable-looking wicker chairs sit in a grassy yard. A basket of knitting materials beside one of the chairs suggests an afternoon of quiet enjoyment spent basking in warm feelings of satisfaction and the beatitude of shared companionship. With this restful and happy image, Rios suggests that the best things in life get even better with age and that romance can only grow sweeter as it ripens.

During the past one hundred years of modernist painting, many important artists have felt it necessary to devote themselves to depicting the angst and instability of contemporary life, often confronting the viewer with shocking images. By contrast, the work of Susan Rios is like a breath of fresh air. To those who would insist that her paintings are escapist, Rios has a well-thought-out answer. "There are terrible pressures in contemporary life, and largely because of the media, our society has focused on how horrible things are in the world. Subsequently, people have lost the ability to recognize that they have a choice about what kind of world they live in. I have a very different philosophy. What I'm saying with my paintings is that you get to choose.

"It's so easy to get caught up in the hustle and bustle and lose out on the best parts of life," she continues. "I want to remind people to pay attention to the good things, to stop and appreciate the small, quiet moments, because they're the most important times in life."

It is this quiet and sincerely life-affirming message that Susan Rios strives to convey with the serene beauty of her art. "To be able to create a positive effect in the world," the artist concludes, "to put something out there that people respond to and find comfort in, that's what is most meaningful for me."

It is one thing to confess to such warm-hearted and lofty aspirations. It is quite another thing to be able to transform them into art.

Susan Rios does both.

Romance Suite:
First Love, 1987
Acrylic, 12 x 14″

Romance Suite:
From This Day Forward, 1987
Acrylic, 12 x 14″

Romance Suite:
The New Arrival, 1987
Acrylic, 14 x 12″

Romance Suite:
Attic Memories, 1987
Acrylic, 12 x 14″

Retreat, 1986
Acrylic, 24 x 30″

The Golden Years, 1987
Acrylic, 14 x 12″

Visiting, 1984
Acrylic, 24 x 26″

Thoughts on a Happy Ending, 1984
Acrylic, 25 x 30"

Intimate Encounters

The theme of intimacy is one of the essential and endearing motifs in the paintings of Susan Rios. She has a special talent for evoking an almost palpable sense of the emotional closeness and warmth that animate encounters between the best of friends and in the best of families. Rather than attempting to show us something so intangible, Rios intelligently employs the power of suggestion, exploring this thematic territory with only indirect and infrequent reference to human figures.

Rios's *Special Visit* invites us to remember and to re-experience moments when deep feelings were shared and appreciated in a thoughtful stillness and in complete trust. The three white wicker chairs appear to have been brought out just for this special occasion, while the coffee cups and books on the table make us think of the pleasure of sharing with a friend. "When I painted *Special Visit,* I imagined an afternoon with friends," says Rios, "one of those incredibly fulfilling times when you have great conversations with people, and you go away feeling fulfilled because you have those friends."

A similarly congenial scene is depicted in *Amaryllis,* one of Rios's best-known works. Two comfortable-looking chairs rest side by side on an enchanting brick patio, while potted amaryllis spring up from a table in the foreground. "I love amaryllis—both the flower and the name," the artist remarks. "I put them in this painting because they're just the type of thing with which I'd like to surround myself and my friends." *Reunion* brings the scene of social interaction inside, yet the open French doors lead us to speculate that the protagonists have just left for a walk around the grounds. The festive brightness of the interior color scheme and the sunny lighting combine to suggest the happiness of the event that has just transpired. And although void of figures, the scene feels alive with Rios's warmly emotional touch.

Rios likes to paint things that are dear to her heart. In *Olivia's Place,* she takes as her subject a tea party thrown by her daughter. "I gave it that title because it's an image of my daughter's tea party; this is her place, which she's set up with her own little name card beside it. And it's also her place in my heart, too." Rios's painting manages to convey both her own maternal feelings as well as the gay conviviality of a young girl's first party.

A slightly more whimsical encounter is featured in *California Picnic.* A family of teddy bears sits on a picnic blanket while a bib-wearing dog displays his best manners, no doubt waiting for the hostess to return with a tray of crumpets and scones. "It's not exactly a heavy subject, but it's a very emotional one," Rios notes, "because it shows the ideal picnic a mother would want for her children."

Secret Time (detail)

Morning Breakfast, 1978
Acrylic, 29½ x 23½″

A Day with Friends, 1985
Acrylic, 36 x 30″

Four O'Clock, 1987
Acrylic, 24 x 30″

Olivia's Place, 1987
Acrylic, 28 x 28″

California Picnic, 1985
Acrylic, 24 x 30″

Together, 1985
Acrylic, 34 x 28″

Among Friends, 1983
Acrylic, 40 x 30″

With My Friends, 1986
Acrylic, 30 x 24″

Secret Time, 1986
Acrylic, 38 x 29″

The Guest Cottage, 1985
Acrylic, 36 x 22″

Grandparent's House, 1984
Acrylic, 28 x 32″

Amaryllis, 1983
Acrylic, 24 x 30″

The Gift Is Yourself, 1985
Acrylic, 24 x 30″

His New York Place, 1978
Acrylic, 40 x 30″

Special Visit, 1985
Acrylic, 30 x 32″

Gardens

Susan Rios delights in creating scenes of great pictorial beauty, and her garden paintings are among her most visually stunning works. Rios feels the same passion for flowers experienced by the great French Impressionist painter Claude Monet (1840–1926). "What I need most of all in life is flowers," remarked Monet. Rios's paintings seem calculated to lead the viewer to a similiar conclusion.

Rios's gardens are not of the clipped hedge variety: instead, lush explosions of colorful flowers sprawl in an overgrown fecundity. Like Monet's renowned garden at Giverny, Rios's garden scenes attempt to duplicate floral beauty in its natural state. "More and more, I get satisfaction in life from things of natural beauty. It seems as if colors in nature never clash with one another—when they interact, they just seem to harmonize. And there's nothing man-made that can can ever reproduce those colors."

As an artist, Rios tackles the challenge of doing just that. *Summer Afternoon* contrasts an array of lavenders, lilacs, blues, yellows, pinks, and reds as well as numerous shades of green; yet the juxtapositions are never in the least jarring. Instead, this sea of color welcomes the eye, and the fluid composition offers an invitingly restful image—this is a garden where one could quietly work out all the problems of the day.

Rios often explores the metaphorical and psychological connotations of gardens. *Peaceful Hours* features an older couple tending their garden: their postures indicate the loving care they bring to this activity and suggest a connection between the special pleasures of cultivating a garden and nurturing a relationship. "Life is so peaceful when you're out in the garden," comments Rios. "So I always imagine that when I get older and I'm probably painting less, I'll find pleasure being among my plants and flowers. Staying inside, it's possible to feel isolated and alone, but in a garden, I always feel at peace with myself. It's truly therapeutic."

Back Garden Gate plays off of a different psychological fantasy—namely, the desire to peek into a private world. Insulated by walls of flowers, Rios's full-blooming gardens have a sanctuarylike quality to them, and in this canvas, curiosity leads us to a view of a neighboring yard. It is an image of a borderline separating two secret worlds, and we take pleasure in trespassing with our eyes.

A breathtakingly picturesque coastal garden is the setting of *Black-Eyed Susans*. Is it set in Cape Cod or Carmel? The white picket fence and the vividly colored garden flowers—as well as the ocean inlet in the background—could have been inspired by either place. "When I made this painting, I imagined the kind of day when the sun is shining, but there's a cool breeze out, and the bright blue sky is streaked with white clouds. It's not too hot out, so it's a perfect day for working in the garden and gazing out at the ocean," explains the artist.

Blackeyed Susans (detail)

Summer Afternoon, 1986
Acrylic, 8 x 10″

Peaceful Hours, 1984
Acrylic, 36 x 40″

A Garden for Vivian, 1984
Acrylic, 24 x 30″

Black-Eyed Susans, 1985
Acrylic, 24 x 30″

Delphiniums, 1986
Acrylic, 25 x 30″

Back Garden Gate, 1986
Acrylic, 10 x 8″

Early Morning, 1986
Acrylic, 26 x 40″

The Hillside Garden, 1984
Acrylic, 34 x 30″

My Garden for Jon, 1986
Acrylic, 28 x 32″

The Garden Collection, 1985
Acrylic, 30 x 32″

The Gardener, *1987*
Acrylic, 30 x 32″

The Other End of the Garden, 1984
Acrylic, 20 x 18″

Behind the Hedge, 1984
Acrylic, 24 x 24″

The Girls' Garden, 1986
Acrylic, 24 x 30″

Loving Touch Suite:
***The Side Garden,** 1987*
Pencil, pen and ink, 14 x 11″

Planting, 1986
Acrylic, 24 x 10″

Everyone Needs Their Garden, 1984
Acrylic, 30 x 32″

Caretaker's Corner, 1987
Acrylic, 10 x 14″

The Garden off the Bedroom, 1978
Acrylic, 24 x 30"

Lilly's Plants, 1984
Acrylic, 30 x 24″

For Susan Rios, romance can take many forms. It can be found in an afternoon stroll through the countryside, in a work of poetry, or in a string of pearls and a flowery white bonnet. By building her compositions around eloquent details, Rios sensitively creates richly emotional atmospheres that seem to brim over with feelings of tenderness.

In *Love Poems,* Rios stages a scene centered around a quietly romantic activity: reading poetry. The lounging cat and the gently diffuse lighting lend a lazy, late afternoon feeling to the image—the perfect moment for daydreaming about a loved one. The painting in the background appears to be an homage to Impressionism—that most romantic of art movements—and the woman's elegant white dress and demure pose enhance the beatific mood of the scene.

Susan Rios presents a more explicitly romantic image in *The Fantasy*. With her back to us, a lithe woman in a diaphanous dress gazes out toward the ocean. Two chairs keep each other company on the beach; their presence suggests an afternoon conversation that still resonates. The idyllic coastal setting would be an ideal spot for a honeymoon, and it is easy to imagine the woman lost in happy visions of a shared future. Although the soft, dreamy tone evinces a definite feminine sensibility, the painting appeals to viewers of both sexes.

With *Afternoon Walk,* Susan Rios turns to the subject of her own marriage. "*Afternoon Walk* expressed my feelings about the future just after Jon and I were married," she recalls. "I pictured us walking through this archway into a future that was bright and sunny and happy." The basket of roses on the wrought-iron bench is a narrative element that, in typical Rios fashion, obliquely describes a previous activity, while the trail of mottled sunlight leads the viewer's eye into the painting's illusionistic depth and in the presumed direction of our newlywed strollers.

Intricately crafted lace fabrics and sensuously blooming flowers also take on a romantic aura in Rios's work. In *The Special Day,* these Rios trademarks are employed to create a delicately subdued portrait of a wedding day. From the dark dresser on the left, a pair of flowers arc across the foreground space so that the two blossoms seem perched just above the fluffy pillows propped up on a virginally white bed. The hatbox and bridal bonnet are quintessential Rios touches: from these intimate details, an entire event is evoked. It is just this type of expansive creativity that epitomizes Susan Rios's romantic accent. Her paintings appeal to everyone who knows that to be truly romantic is to invent one's own world.

The Fantasy (detail)

Love Poems, 1986
Acrylic, 32 x 30″

The Fantasy, 1986
Acrylic, 32 x 30"

Afternoon Walk, 1985
Acrylic, 34 x 24″

The Special Day, 1986
Acrylic, 30 x 24″

For Love, 1985
Acrylic, 26 x 34″

Thinking About It, 1983
Acrylic, 34 x 34″

Alice, 1985
Acrylic, 30 x 25″

For Terry, 1984
Acrylic, 28 x 32″

A Place with J, *1985*
Acrylic, 28 x 32″

Success, 1984
Acrylic, 30 x 24″

Their Vacation Place, 1986
Acrylic, 24 x 32″

Summer Morning, 1987
Pencil, pen and ink, 11 x 14″

Susan Rios's interior scenes welcome the viewer to an old-fashioned world full of grace and charm. Rios's cozily cluttered rooms often remind us of places we have known and make us yearn for similar environments. A conflation of invention and documentary details, these bright, sunny interiors would seem at home anywhere from New England to California. Ultimately, they are places of the heart.

The intensity of feeling invested in these scenes allows them to adopt an almost allegorical dimension. *Coming Home* presents an image of a cheerful living room decorated with floral motifs and a Renoir-like painting on the rear wall. But the sense of comfort and peace that emanates from this painting goes beyond merely decorative concerns. Says Rios: "I chose the title to convey the sense of coming home to the best part of yourself. I think home is a nice place we have inside of ourselves, and sometimes a warm, friendly room like this one can help us get back there."

In *The Coast House,* Rios creates a snugly comfortable interior that starkly contrasts with the gray, stormy-looking seascape depicted in the background windows. The wintry light assures us that this is the perfect kind of day to curl up on the couch with a soft blanket and a wonderful novel. *The Guest House* suggests a more summery clime, as French doors open out onto a back garden. This commingling of interior and exterior characterizes many of Rios's domestic scenes: there is a sense in these paintings that one can move freely from indoors to outdoors. The abundance of flowers included in these images—whether actual flowers in vases or floral designs on the upholstery and wallpaper—similarly suggests a commingling of interior and exterior. As with Rios's garden paintings, there is a sense of communication and harmony between culture and nature.

Perhaps the only interior scene in Rios's oeuvre that includes an image of technology is the drawing *His Afternoon*. An old gramophone sits on a table behind a couch covered with ornately patterned pillows. Colorfully bound books have been casually stacked on the rug—within easy reaching distance of the supine reader we can imagine spending a leisurely afternoon listening to music and consulting favorite texts. Details such as the intricate design of the rug are lovingly crafted: Rios claims that she will paint a single pillow as many as six times before she is satisfied with the result. It is precisely this kind of devoted attention to detail that infuses Rios's interiors with their vivid aura of warmth and hospitality.

Olivia and I (detail)

Table with Two Odd Chairs, 1977
Acrylic, 36 x 30″

The Yellow Chair and Rose, 1977
Acrylic, 28 x 22″

Morning View of the Garden, 1978
Acrylic, 41 x 31″

Coming Home, 1985
Acrylic, 30 x 34″

The Coast House, 1984
Acrylic, 34 x 30″

Olivia and I, 1984
Acrylic, 30 x 34″

The Guest House, 1986
Acrylic, 30 x 32″

His Afternoon, 1987
Pencil, pen and ink, 14 x 11″

Marybeth and I, 1984
Acrylic, 36 x 30″

A Visit with Susan, 1986
Acrylic, 26 x 28″

A Corner of the Library, 1984
Acrylic, 36 x 30″

Orchids, 1984
Acrylic, 24 x 24″

Elizabeth's Corner, 1984
Acrylic, 20 x 18″

The Room off the Terrace, 1987
Pencil, pen and ink, 14 x 11″

Country House Suite:
The Wisconsin House, *1987*
Pencil, pen and ink, 11½ x 14½″

Places Suite:
In the Cottage, *1987*
Pencil, pen and ink, 14 x 11″

Country House Suite:
Plant Tending Day, *1987*
Pencil, pen and ink, 14 x 11″

The Art of Solitude

Susan Rios's images remind us of the importance of quiet contemplation and reflection; her paintings conjure up a world where solitude can be delightfully enjoyed. In *Planning the Future,* the composition is centered around a comfortable-looking wicker divan and a casually rumpled red blanket that still seems to hold the warmth of whomever it was just covering. The painting on the back wall adds an exotic element: a woman clad in elegant Asian clothing brings to mind distant places that are mysterious and appealing. "Planning the future is the moment when your life expands to include new possibilities," Rios comments. "Instead of feeling as if you're looking down a narrow tunnel, you see into a brighter future where you can imagine your dreams coming true. It's the time when you feel the best about yourself—there's peace and space inside, and you can radiate out."

Rios likes to portray scenes in which it is easy to imagine being comfortably alone, completely absorbed in a daydream or some meditative pastime. *My Corner* depicts an inviting scene warmly lit with the late afternoon sun. "This is one of the few paintings I've based on a real place. That's the spot where I sit reading the mail each day. It's a relaxing time I always cherish." In *After Breakfast,* Rios presents a single white wicker chair beside a table just big enough to hold a book, a vase of flowers, and a tea cup. In the background, a cozy inlet opens up to a horizon of sea and sky. "My concept was of a place where you had gone for a visit," says Rios, "and you have stepped out there to look at the ocean, to read your book, and to think."

The title *Finding Peace with Yourself* says it all. With this painting, Rios presents an exterior scene that exudes a sense of quiet and privacy. The elegant hammock, the chair, and the tea setting, as well as the open volume on the grass, seem to leave no conceivable desires unprovided for. *Finding Peace with Yourself* is an image that reminds us of the need to spend quality time with ourselves, to find that centered feeling Rios evokes with such heart-felt eloquence.

After Breakfast (detail)

Planning the Future, 1986
Acrylic, 32 x 30"

My Corner, 1986
Acrylic, 26 x 32″

After Breakfast, *1986*
Acrylic, 30 x 24″

Finding Peace with Yourself, 1985
Acrylic, 28 x 38″

The Private Spot, 1986
Acrylic, 30 x 24″

Alone Comfortably, 1984
Acrylic, 30 x 25″

An Hour with Emily Dickinson, 1984
Acrylic, 24 x 32″

To Cultivate a Friendship, 1984
Acrylic, 32 x 28″

That One Afternoon, 1984
Acrylic, 32 x 28″

Marguerite Rose, 1984
Acrylic, 10 x 8″

The Thinking Spot, 1987
Pencil, pen and ink, 14 x 11″

Allison's Corner, 1987
Pencil, pen and ink, 14 x 11″

Birthday Afternoon, 1987
Pencil, pen and ink, 14½ x 11½″

Memories of Anna, 1987
Acrylic, 10 x 14″

Among Rios's most poignant scenes are her images of public places: flower shops, antique stores, and Victorian inns. As with her other paintings, these images convey a wonderful intimacy: they seem secreted away in a world of their own, captured in a special moment of privileged access. And always they seem like places we would love to visit.

Lilacs and Lace presents a quaint-looking storefront with windows featuring an inventory of the treasured artifacts found in other Rios paintings. "I wanted to put all those nice things in the window so you'd feel like this was a store you would just love to walk into," says Rios. "Originally, the architectural details were inspired by a photograph of a little house with virtually no foliage. I added all the details to create the kind of environment that says, 'Come in and look around.'"

Phoebe's was initially inspired by a the exterior of a bar in Carmel. Rios re-worked the architectural design to create her lovely homage to the flower shop. Like Rios's more private images, *Phoebe's* possesses an elusive familiarity: the scene portrayed elicits an immediate response of recognition, yet it could be set anywhere from London to Monterey. *Phoebe's* is one of Rios's rare canvases that includes a human figure: through the door to the shop, a young woman is posed with her face turned to the side as if she were occupied with arranging some stunning bouquet.

Warm afternoon sunlight invests *Emily's Inn* with the restful stillness of a sleepy summer day. Rios clearly delights in the lighting effects in this painting as much as she does in re-creating the front of a wonderful-looking inn, replete with gingerbread trim and blossoming rose bushes. "Cape May is an incredibly beautiful town on the New Jersey coast filled with old Victorian hotels and cozy places like this one. As in *Cape May, Emily's Inn* is based on one of the photographs I took during a visit there. With *Emily's Inn,* I wanted to do a closeup of Cape May in order to create a more specific image of a place where it would be delightful to stay."

Rios also paints scenes that treat the theme of visiting one's neighbors. These images fill out the novelistic world suggested by Rios's oeuvre; they give us a sense of characters exploring a specific geographical place, and they provide an imaginary neighborhood context for Rios's more privately domestic images. *Visiting* takes us down an overgrown path leading to a flagstone house partially shielded by blossoming flora. Rios focuses her composition around an empty space: the light-colored stone terrace that presumably leads to an entryway. Consequently, the painting evokes that enjoyable anticipation experienced on approaching a familiar place where we know we will find good friends. "Friends are among the truly important things in life," says Rios. "My images are often inspired by particular friends and the places where they live. To me, those are very special places."

Beyond the Footbridge (detail)

Beyond the Footbridge, 1986
Acrylic, 30 x 24"

The Stone Cottage, 1978
Acrylic, 30 x 40″

Emily's Inn, *1986*
Acrylic, 30 x 24″

Fiona s, 1984
Acrylic, 32 x 28″

Down the Lane to Your House, 1984
Acrylic, 24 x 26″

Thy Neighbor's Garden, 1985
Acrylic, 32 x 28"

Mark's Cottage, 1985
Acrylic, 32 x 26″

Lilacs and Lace, 1985
Acrylic, 30 x 36″

Phoebe's, 1984
Acrylic, 34 x 32″

Future, 1985
Acrylic, 32 x 30″

The Stone Barn, 1978
Acrylic, 30 x 26″

Still lifes have been an enduring motif throughout art history. While some of Rios's subjects, such as a vase of flowers or a table setting, possess a timeless quality, they are also extremely personal. "I put things that appeal to me in my paintings," says Rios. "Things like blue and white china, wicker and lace. That's why my work has such a personal appeal: many people enjoy things that give me satisfaction and peace of mind, and there's not any way I could ever make those things seem impersonal."

From the Garden includes all of Rios's favorite elements in a simple, yet perfectly composed scene. It is an image that produces a calming effect: the gentle lighting and cheerful color scheme combine to evoke a sunny tranquility. Rios exercises her delight in painting china in *Tea in the Greenhouse*. The intricate and elaborate design of the various cups and teapots, as well as the lace tablecloth, take us back to a world where things were handmade and crafted with individual detail. *A Short Story* displays Rios's narrative virtuosity: the frozen tableau seems to bring to life the contents of a delightful children's book.

Rios often treats still life subjects in her drawings. Like *The Workbench,* an image inspired by Rios's experience working in a flower shop, these drawings seem like details abstracted from larger paintings. "Drawings allow me more freedom," comments Rios. "I like to use drawings to do closeups or little vignettes in a way that's different from the paintings. With the drawings the space around the image is as important as what's in it."

My Old Studio (detail)

From the Garden, 1983
Acrylic, 36 x 30″

Tea in the Greenhouse, 1984
Acrylic, 20 x 24″

A Short Story, 1984
Acrylic, 20 x 20″

The Workbench, *1987*
Pencil, pen and ink, 14½ x 11½″

Mary G., *1984*
Acrylic, 10 x 8″

Portrait of Theodora, 1984
Acrylic, 20 x 20″

Loving Touch Suite:
The Gardener's Table, *1987*
Pencil, pen and ink, 11 x 14″

Loving Touch Suite:
Fiona's Collection, 1987
Pencil, pen and ink, 14 x 11"

Mary Louise's Shawl, 1987
Pencil, pen and ink, 14 x 11"

The Pisces Plate, 1987
Pencil, pen and ink, 11½ x 14½″

Bird Lover's Guide, 1987
Pencil, pen and ink, 14 x 11″

PLACES SUITE:
The Collector, 1987
Pencil, pen and ink, 14 x 11″

COUNTRY HOUSE SUITE:
Mother's Day, 1987
Pencil, pen and ink, 11 x 14″

My Old Studio, 1979
Acrylic, 40 x 30″

Catalogue Raisonné

The following images were all published as original serigraphs, in limited editions hand-signed by the artist. Edition sizes below are exclusive of Artist's Proofs, Printer's Proofs, Hors Commerce, etc. Asterisk indicates editions published by Naif International. All others are publications of Martin Lawrence Limited Editions. Dimensions are given in inches.

Her Time, 1987
370*
33 x 30

Garden Room, 1987
370*
30 x 29

Fionas, 1984
295
35 x 30

Amaryllis, 1983
295
30 x 35

Peaceful Hours, 1984
295
34¼ x 36¼

Sunday Morning, 1984
295
35 x 33

Reunion, 1984
295
34 x 37

Phoebe's, 1984
295
32 x 30

Afternoon Walk, 1985
295
37 x 32

Special Visit, 1985
295
37 x 38

Main Street, 1985
295
36 x 30

Lilacs and Lace, 1985
295
37 x 42

Planning the Future, 1986
295
35 x 32

After Breakfast, 1986
295
35¼ x 29¼

Coming Home, 1987
295
37¾ x 40

Our House, 1987
295
37½ x 44

Grampa's House, 1987
295
35 x 38

My Corner, 1987
295
33 x 38

Visiting, 1987
295
34 x 35

That Delightful Chat, 1988
295
40¾ x 35¾

Emily's Inn, 1988
295
40¼ x 33

ROMANCE SUITE:
First Love, 1988
295
18 x 20

ROMANCE SUITE:
From This Day Forward, 1988
295
18 x 20

ROMANCE SUITE:
The New Arrival, 1988
295
20 x 18

ROMANCE SUITE:
Attic Memories, 1988
295
20 x 18

Offset Lithographs

The following images have been reproduced by Martin Lawrence Limited Editions as Fine Art Posters. Dimensions are given in inches.

Visiting, 1984
36 x 27

Among Friends, 1986
34 x 24

Last Dance, 1988
40 x 33

Exhibition History

ONE-WOMAN SHOWS

1979	Salon des Independents	Palm Springs, CA
	The Staircase	Beverly Hills, CA
1982	Serendipity Gallery	Los Angeles, CA
1983	Serendipity Gallery	Los Angeles, CA
	Serendipity Gallery	Palos Verdes, CA
1984	Martin Lawrence Galleries	Los Angeles, CA
	Martin Lawrence Galleries	Newport Beach, CA
	Hallowell Gallery	Philadelphia, PA
1985	Martin Lawrence Galleries	Newport Beach, CA
	Martin Lawrence Galleries	Brentwood, CA
1986	Chabot Galleries	Campbell, CA
	Martin Lawrence Galleries	Los Angeles, CA
	Martin Lawrence Galleries	Sherman Oaks, CA
	Martin Lawrence Galleries	Short Hills, NJ
1987	Galleria Prova	Tokyo, Japan
	Martin Lawrence Galleries	West Los Angeles, CA
	Martin Lawrence Galleries	Redondo Beach, CA
	Martin Lawrence Galleries	Santa Clara, CA
	Martin Lawrence Galleries	Thousand Oaks, CA
	Martin Lawrence Galleries	Brentwood, CA
	Martin Lawrence Galleries	Newport Beach, CA
	Martin Lawrence Galleries	Palm Springs, CA
	Martin Lawrence Galleries	Escondido, CA
1988	Billy Hork Galleries	Chicago, IL
	Bloch Gallery	Marblehead, MA
	Emporium Enterprises	Dallas, TX
	Hoitts Gallery	San Francisco, CA
	Moyal Gallery	Dallas, TX
	Martin Lawrence Galleries	West Los Angeles, CA
	Martin Lawrence Galleries	Redondo Beach, CA
	Martin Lawrence Galleries	Santa Clara, CA
	Martin Lawrence Galleries	Thousand Oaks, CA
	Martin Lawrence Galleries	Brentwood, CA
	Martin Lawrence Galleries	Newport Beach, CA
	Martin Lawrence Galleries	Palm Springs, CA
	Martin Lawrence Galleries	Escondido, CA
	Martin Lawrence Galleries	Corte Madera, CA
	Martin Lawrence Galleries	Santa Ana, CA
	Martin Lawrence Galleries	Mission Valley, CA
	Martin Lawrence Galleries	Palm Desert, CA
	Nancy Teague	Seattle, WA
	Newbury Fine Arts	Boston, MA
	Petrini Art Galleries	Hartford, CT
	Martin Lawrence Galleries	Short Hills, NJ
	Martin Lawrence Galleries	Philadelphia, PA
	Martin Lawrence Galleries	Soho, NY
	Martin Lawrence Galleries	Baltimore, MD
	Martin Lawrence Galleries	Glen Burnie, NY
	Martin Lawrence Galleries	Princeton, NJ
	Martin Lawrence Galleries	Washington, DC
	Reid Gallery	Carmel, CA
	Renjeau Galleries	Natick, MA
	Warwick Gallery	Warwick, RI

GROUP EXHIBITIONS

1980	L.A. Art Association	Los Angeles, CA
	Balboa Bay Club	Newport Beach, CA
	Designers Adcock/Stock	Los Angeles, CA
1981	New York Art Expo	New York, NY
	Galleria La Costa	Carlsbad, CA
1982	New York Art Expo	New York, NY
1984	Martin Lawrence Galleries	Los Angeles, CA
	Martin Lawrence Galleries	Newport Beach, CA
	New York Art Expo	New York, NY
	Hallowell Gallery	Philadelphia, PA
1985	New York Art Expo	New York, NY
1986	New York Art Expo	New York, NY
	Galleria Prova	Tokyo, Japan
1987	Gallery Sho	Tokyo, Japan
1988	Newbury Fine Arts	Boston, MA
	Galleria Prova	Tokyo, Japan
	Orange Coast Art	Fountain Valley, CA
	Petrini Art Galleries	Hartford, CT
	Reid Gallery	Carmel, CA
	Renjeau Galleries	Natick, MA
	Steffaninos Gallery	Costa Mesa, CA
	Universal Fine Art	Redmond, WA
	Carlson Galleries	Dallas, TX
	Esprit Decor	Phoenix, AZ
	Gallery Victoria Mann	Sunriver, CA
	Graphics Galore	Phoenix, AZ
	Masters Gallery	Scottsdale, AZ
	Picture Gallery	Salem, NH
	Bishops Gallery	San Diego, CA
	Gallery LeShea	Santa Barbara, CA

Index of Illustrations

Italic numerals indicate text references.

Contributing Editor
Elliot Blinder

Produced by
Perpetua Press, Los Angeles

Designed by
Dana Levy

Typeset in Schneidler by
Continental Typographics, Chatsworth, Ca

Display type set in
Young Baroque
an alphabet designed by Doyald Young

Printed by
Dai Nippon Printing Co., Tokyo